PHILADELPHIA BIG 5

TO John:
Enjoy the History!

PHILADELPHIA BIG 5

M. EARL SMITH

ARCADIA
PUBLISHING

Copyright © 2018 by M. Earl Smith
ISBN 978-1-4671-2980-0

Published by Arcadia Publishing
Charleston, South Carolina

Printed in the United States of America

Library of Congress Control Number: 2018935926

For all general information, please contact Arcadia Publishing:
Telephone 843-853-2070
Fax 843-853-0044
E-mail sales@arcadiapublishing.com
For customer service and orders:
Toll-Free 1-888-313-2665

Visit us on the Internet at www.arcadiapublishing.com

CONTENTS

ACKNOWLEDGMENTS

Every time I write a book for Arcadia, the work gets easier. This is a testament to the great minds that work for the publisher, whose dedication to their craft is unrivaled in the publishing business. Erin Vosgien, who has been a wonderful sounding board for the many ideas I have for volumes about my favorite towns along the eastern seaboard, must be the first person thanked. I also must thank Caroline Anderson, whose editorial eye and calm disposition are a port in the storm that is writing a book. Leigh Scott, Adam Kidd, Jonny Foster, Dani McGrath, Jordan Crisp, and Megan Petrie have done an incredible amount of work promoting my works, and for that, I thank them.

Special thanks go to my contacts in the athletic departments at each school featured in this book: Mike Mahoney at Penn, Larry Dougherty at Temple, Dan Lobcaz at La Salle, Mike Sheridan at Villanova, and Dominick DiJulia at Saint Joseph's. The materials, background, and contacts that each of you provided for this volume were an invaluable asset to its creation. I would also like to thank Temple's John Baum, Villanova's Dr. Ed Hastings, La Salle's Bill Bradshaw, Penn's Steve Bilsky, and Saint Joseph's Dominick DiJulia for their wonderful chapter introductions, which give a great insider's perspective into the Big 5.

On a personal note, the list of people who helped me is, as always, too long to include everyone, but I am going to try. Nick, Leah, and Lydia: Pop loves you, and I hope you love this! To my long list of coauthors and illustrators, Jade Huguenot, Maggie Rymsza, Nayeli Riano, and Gus Ferres: I have loved working with all of you and thank you for the honor. Finally, to Kate Syndes, for watching Che, the greatest Sheltie in the world, while I mucked around archives in the Keystone State.

Unless otherwise noted, all images are from the author's personal collection.

INTRODUCTION

Unlike most of the books I have composed for Arcadia Publishing and their varied local history series, this one was on a subject that I had some personal experience with. No, I never played in the Big 5; my playing days for any sport ended during my high school years, and the thought of a plodder like me playing at the highest level that college basketball had to offer is laughable. My connection to the pageantry and lore of the Big 5 came as a student. In my first semester at Penn (2015–2016), I was introduced to one of the joys of being on campus: free tickets! I was struggling, at 32, to fit into an environment that consisted of a bunch of students who I claimed 10 years of seniority over, yet nothing brings people closer together than the triumph of a shared sports team. As I write this, Philadelphia fans are preparing to celebrate their first professional football championship since 1960, and all the Big 5 schools have canceled classes to take part.

On December 28, 2015, a group of fellow nontraditional students and I took a short road trip (I was the only one on campus with a car, so my decrepit Honda puttered us all down I-476) to see Penn take on the eventual national champion Villanova Wildcats at The Pavilion. The fact that we were playing Villanova puzzled me. Aside from being close in distance, there was little in common between the Catholic ballers who made up the Wildcats and the Ivy League kids known as the Quakers. Penn sits in the heart of West Philadelphia and lays claim to 24,000 students, along with Pennsylvania's largest medical network, all while employing the largest workforce in the mid-Atlantic. Villanova, on the other hand, sits outside the consolidated Philadelphia area, boasts half the student body size of Penn . . . and yet lays claim to three times as many national championships.

Penn was of no benefit to Villanova in the area of exposure, nor could our paltry 11-17 record against admittedly inferior competition be of any benefit to Villanova's RPI (rating percentage index). So why were we there? I asked one person in my group, who happened to be the son of a Penn employee, a long-termer who was also a graduate.

My friend laughed. "It's the Big 5!" he exclaimed, as if that explained everything.

In this era of cell phones and instant information, I was quick to my phone (once, of course, I had stopped driving). What I read was fascinating. A local, round-robin tournament, played for little save bragging rights, that dated back almost 70 years? It reminded me of some of my high school football rivalries against either private schools that recruited or public schools that were in smaller districts than us, played for little more than local pride and bragging rights.

I fell instantly in love. Given how my Quakers are a non-scholarship program, the odds of us winning a national championship are thin, and, while the rivalries of the Ivy League are intense across all sports, the idea of playing for the championship of Philadelphia, given its status as the home of America's independence, was appealing. No, it was more than appealing. It was exhilarating.

That thrill lives on in every Big 5 game. I have had the honor of seeing several now, games involving many different combinations of teams in each arena that can lay claim to hosting this hallowed tradition, and each and every Big 5 game has a little something extra. The players push harder, the fans cheer louder, the coaches pour every bit of passion and strategy into all 40 minutes of game time, almost desperate, it seems, to stake their claim as the best of Philadelphia.

In the modern era of big-money college sports, when state-run institutions hold an advantage because admission standards are lower and budgets are bigger, the Big 5 remains a unique jewel in the college sports landscape. If you think about it, aside from geography, what is the appeal? You have five private schools, three of which are Catholic, one Baptist, and one Quaker, finding common ground on the court. Every demographic of Philadelphia is represented: La Salle and Saint Joseph's are truly modern titans of inner-city universities, Penn has its ivory towers and prime real estate, Temple provides a massive opportunity to a diverse population of students, and Villanova reminds the city that there are brilliant minds and athletes beyond its imaginary borders.

In short, these five schools represent the best of college sports. When athletes are unpaid, you tend to see the purest representation of the game, and this pure representation puts another notch in the belt of Philadelphia, one of the best cities in the world and one of the biggest sports towns in America. From Joe Frazier to the Phillies, from the world champion Eagles to the ghosts of Extreme Championship Wrestling, and from the Flyers, to the 76ers, to the Soul, to the Union, to Army-Navy, and, yes, to the Big 5, Philadelphia represents what is best about American sports.

As a Penn alum, I proudly say, "Go Quakers!" As a fan of the Big 5, I also say, "Go Wildcats!", "Go Owls!", "Go Explorers!", and "Go Hawks!"

As long as they are not playing the Quakers.

One

THE LA SALLE UNIVERSITY EXPLORERS

La Salle men's basketball—for many in the Philadelphia Big 5 and college basketball world, it means a long-storied history with a strong tradition like few others. For many La Salle alumni, it means everything. They eat, sleep, and breathe Explorer basketball and are some of the most die-hard and passionate fans in college basketball.

And with good reason. Most agree that men's basketball is what first put La Salle College on the map.

Since its inaugural 1930–1931 season, the history of La Salle basketball is filled with amazing stories, dedicated coaches, top-notch teams, legendary players, and, for the alumni who witnessed it all, unforgettable memories.

The names roll off the tongue: Tom Gola, Larry Cannon, Ken Durrett, Michael Brooks, Lionel Simmons. All five had their jerseys retired by La Salle, and they might be the greatest five players any college basketball program has ever produced. Yet they are not alone.

Who can forget seeing Ralph Lewis and Donnie Carr? How about Joe "Jellybean" Bryant and Randy Woods? Or Larry Foust, an eight-time National Basketball Association (NBA) All-Star? Tim Legler, Bill Raftery, Doug Overton, Steven Smith, and Rasual Butler . . . the list goes on and on.

La Salle has two national championship teams—the 1952 National Invitational Tournament (NIT) champions (considered the top tournament of college basketball at the time), and the 1954 National Collegiate Athletic Association (NCAA) tournament champions. The 1968–1969 team, with four future NBA players in the starting lineup, finished with a 23-1 record and ranked second in the final Associated Press poll.

The school has also had its share of Hall of Fame coaches, like Ken Loeffler and Speedy Morris. Fran Dunphy, a player on the renowned 1968–1969 squad, has been a legendary college coach at Temple and Penn. Paul Westhead coached at La Salle in the 1970s and has won an NBA title as the head coach of the Los Angeles Lakers and a Women's National Basketball Association (WNBA) title with the Phoenix Mercury.

La Salle men's basketball has a history that rivals any college basketball program in the country. The Explorers have been ranked nationally a remarkable 111 times since the 1950s, boast three National Players of the Year, won an NCAA tournament championship and an NIT championship, and have had 22 players go on to play in the NBA. Philadelphia is one of the best and most historic college basketball cities anywhere, and La Salle basketball is a significant part of this storied tradition.

—Bill Bradshaw
Athletic director, La Salle University (BS, La Salle, 1969)

College Hall is the main administrative building on the campus of La Salle University (formerly La Salle College), a private Roman Catholic institution founded in 1863. It is one of three Catholic-founded universities in the Big 5 (along with Saint Joseph's and Villanova). College Hall forms the north side of the quadrangle and houses many of the administrative offices, and is the hub of instruction.

Connelly Library is located at 1900 Onley Avenue. Among other things, the library hosts in its special collections the largest collection of Vietnam-era propaganda in the world, a unique assemblage on the academic and historical works of Nobel Prize laureate Bob Dylan, and several editions of the Bible dating from the 15th century.

The La Salle University Student Union was constructed in the 1950s. It is currently home to several storefront dining options. The Student Union, a beautiful and modern structure, houses student meeting rooms, dining rooms, the college store, ballroom, a theater, and many other facilities for student service.

This photograph was taken during the 1950–1951 season, which was tainted by several betting scandals. The text on the back reads "Enthusiasm at a low pitch: New York; With the cloud of basketball "fixes" hanging in the air, only several thousand fans appeared in Madison Square Garden for the early part of the Manhattan–La Salle game, Feb. 20. La Salle won this game, 64-63. In the second game, St. John's defeated NYU, 61-52." La Salle would finish the season 22-7, with a 3-1 record in the Big 5.

Personal tragedy can sometimes overlap what happens on the court. The caption for this press photograph reads, "Philadelphia, March 31—Will not play against—Jackie Moore, La Salle College basketball star, whose mother died here today, said he was too broken up over her death to even think of basketball and would not play in tonight's semi-final Olympic trial game against Kansas. Coach Ken Loeffler said his team would be badly crippled without Moore." For the 1952 season, La Salle finished 24-5, with a win in the NIT and a 4-1 record against Big 5 opponents.

Shown here is perhaps one of the greatest basketball players in NCAA history, Tom Gola. The arena at La Salle carries his name. Gola led the Explorers to a 1952 NIT championship, a 1954 NCAA championship, and a runner-up finish in the 1955 NCAA tournament. Although the Big 5 did not become an official league until a year after Gola's graduation, Gola-led teams would finish 13-2 against Big 5 opponents during his time as a player. Gola coached the Explorers for two seasons, leading the team to a 23-1 record during the 1968–1969 season, including a Big 5 championship with a 4-0 record.

This is the 1953–1954 national champion La Salle Explorers. The Explorers finished the season 26-4, including a 3-1 record against future Big 5 opponents. From left to right are (first row) Frank Blatcher, Bob Maples, Frank O'Hara, Tom Gola, and Bob Ames; (second row) Chuck Greenberg, Fran O'Malley, John Yodsnukis, Charles Singley, and manager John Moosbugger. The Explorers beat Fordham, North Carolina State, Navy, Penn State, and, in the finals, Bradley. (Courtesy of the La Salle Athletic Department.)

One year later, the Explorers, under the watchful eye of superstar Tom Gola (shown here shortly before his death), would nearly repeat their NCAA success. The team finished with a 26-5 record, going 2-0 against their Big 5 opponents. They made their way to the NCAA championship game only to fall to the University of San Francisco, a fellow Catholic institution, by a score of 77-63. Gola was drafted third overall by his hometown Philadelphia Warriors in the 1955 NBA draft. He won an NBA title in his rookie season, made five all-star teams, and was enshrined into the Naismith Memorial Basketball Hall of Fame in 1976. (Courtesy of the La Salle Athletic Department.)

La Salle Hall of Famer Lawrence "Larry" Cannon is pictured when he played for the Denver Rockets. In his time with the Explorers, Cannon was twice an All-American, while averaging almost 19 points per game. He was inducted into the Philadelphia Big 5 Hall of Fame in 1973. Averaging 16.6 points per season as a professional, Cannon led the Indiana Pacers to an American Basketball Association (ABA) title. A strong professional career was cut short by a condition known as phlebitis, an inflammation of veins; in this case, in his legs.

Shown signing autographs for some young fans is former La Salle all-star Joe Bryant. Bryant spent two years at La Salle carving enough of a legacy that he was drafted in the first round of the 1975 NBA draft. Bryant spent eight seasons in the NBA before embarking on a coaching career that took him to Boston, Thailand, Japan, and back to La Salle, where he was an assistant coach until 1996. That year, he resigned to help manage the NBA career of his son, Kobe Bryant. The Explorers won the Big 5 in 1974–1975, his senior season.

This pocket schedule shows the fall and winter slates for each of the 1977 teams at La Salle, including the women's and men's basketball teams. On the men's side, the Explorers finished 17-12, which included a 2-2 record in Big 5 games. This included wins over Saint Joseph's and Big 5 co-champion Temple and losses to Villanova and Big 5 co-champion Penn. On the women's side, the Explorers finished 14-8 and played each of their Big 5 counterparts. The schools also faced each other in a Big 5 cross-country meet, while the Explorers played Big 5 teams in men's soccer, women's volleyball, women's field hockey, and women's volleyball.

Shown is the gravesite of Robert Ames (known as Bob Ames during his Explorer days, when he was a member of the 1953–1954 national championship team). He joined the US Army in 1956, shortly after his playing days ended, then left the Army to join the CIA, rising to the rank of director of Near East Intelligence. Sadly, Ames perished in the 1983 embassy bombing in Beirut, Lebanon, at the relatively young age of 49. Pres. Ronald Reagan attended his funeral. (Courtesy of the La Salle Athletic Department.)

FALL SPORTS 1982

Several Big 5 opponents were on the schedule for the various fall sports teams of the La Salle Explorers in 1982. The men's soccer team faced all four Big 5 schools, while in October of that year, the men's cross-country teams from each school participated in the Big 5 Meet. The women's cross-country teams held a Big 5 Meet of their own, while the women Explorers faced Temple, Saint Joseph's, and Villanova. In women's volleyball, the Explorers clashed with Saint Joseph's and Villanova, while in tennis, the Explorers only managed to work in Villanova.

La Salle coach Bill "Speedy" Morris was, among other achievements, the first coach in NCAA history to coach both the men's and women's programs at the same school, which he did at La Salle. Morris coached the Explorers to 238 wins, including a 30-2 season behind Lionel Simmons in 1989–1990. Morris won four Big 5 titles as a coach (1989, 1990, 1992, and 1998). Today, he is the head coach of St. Joseph's Preparatory School in Philadelphia, where he is currently in pursuit of his 1,000th win as a prep head coach.

The 1989–1990 season was one of the most successful in the history of La Salle basketball, even if it did end with a loss in the second round of the NCAA tournament. Led by two-time consensus All-American and Naismith College Player of the Year Lionel Simmons, the Explorers went 30-2, with Simmons averaging 24.6 points and 10.9 rebounds per game. La Salle went 16-0 in Metro Atlantic Athletic Conference (MAAC) play, won the conference's tournament, and went 5-0 in Big 5 games, although three of those (Penn, Temple, and Villanova) were won by a combined five points.

One of the greatest to ever play in the Big 5, Lionel Simmons's legacy will not soon be forgotten. Aside from leading La Salle to two Big 5 titles (1989 and 1990), Simmons led La Salle to a 30-2 record, a No. 1 ranking, and the second round of the NCAA tournament during the 1989–1990 season. Simmons was a four-time All–Big 5 player, and three times received the Robert V. Geasey Trophy, given annually to the most outstanding player in the Big 5. Simmons went on to be selected seventh overall by the Sacramento Kings, where he was named to the NBA All-Rookie Team and played seven seasons before retiring.

Guarding French league all-star Landing Sane is La Salle legend Rodney Green (in blue). Green spent four years with the Explorers (2006–2010) and left as the ninth all-time leading scorer, with 1,914 points. He was twice named All–Atlantic 10, as well as being named to three All–Big 5 teams. In an ironic twist of disappointment, the Explorers failed to win the Big 5 in any of his four seasons. Since graduation, Green has played professionally in France, Hungary, Israel, Italy, Poland, Ukraine, and Argentina.

Shown here playing in the French LBA Pro A league is La Salle Explorers legend Steven Smith. Smith was twice named Atlantic 10 Player of the Year (2005 and 2006) along with two All–Atlantic 10 selections. While the Explorers were unable to win a Big 5 title during his time at La Salle, it has not deterred his career. After some time with the NBA's Philadelphia 76ers, Smith has played professionally overseas in Spain, Greece, Italy, France, Germany, and Israel. His Greek team won the Greek Cup in 2012.

The 2002–2003 season was not much better for the Explorers. On the men's side, La Salle finished 12-17, including a record of 0-5 in Big 5 play. On December 7, 2002, the Explorers fell to Villanova 74-71. On January 28, 2003, the Explorers fell to Penn 79-66. On February 24, the Explorers fell to Saint Joseph's 75-53 (and would also lose to the Hawks 68-48 in the second round of the Atlantic 10 tournament). Finally, the Explorers lost to Temple 68-58, on March 6. On the women's side, the Explorers finished a pedestrian 15-14, including a 1-3 record in Big 5 play, with their lone win coming against Penn.

The 2006–2007 season was a rough one for the Explorers, as they would finish with a dismal 10-20 and 14th place in the Atlantic 10. The Big 5 did not go much better for the Explorers; at 0-4, they finished in last place. On December 23, the Explorers fell to Villanova 64-51. On January 18, the Explorers fell to Penn 93-92. On February 4, Temple blew out La Salle 89-64. Finally, on February 10, the Explorers lost to Saint Joseph's by a tally of 72-50.

The game between La Salle and Penn on January 18, 2007, was one of the greatest Big 5 games in recent memory. The 2006–2007 season was not a successful one for the Explorers. The Quakers, on the other hand, finished with a 22-9 record, an Ivy League championship, and an NCAA tournament berth. None of that mattered, however, as city pride brought out the best in both teams, leading to a thrilling 93-92 barn-burning win for the Quakers at Tom Gola Arena. The teams traded the lead 15 times and tied five more in the final 13:26 minutes. Games like this show why the Big 5 is important.

On the women's side, the Explorers fared much better in the 2006–2007 season. The team finished 19-11 in coach Tom Lochner's third season. The Explorers made it to the semifinals of the Atlantic 10 tournament, where they were bounced by a Cinderella Dayton team by a score of 57-43. In Big 5 play, the Explorers finished 2-2, with wins over Villanova (74-52) and Penn (73-63) and losses to Temple (68-55) and Saint Joseph's (71-60).

The 2012–2013 season was an unexpected bright point for the Explorers, as they stormed to a 24-10 record, including an 11-5 record in the Atlantic 10. After losing in the conference quarterfinals, the Explorers received an at-large bid to the NCAA field of 68 as one of the eight play-in teams. The Explorers played their way all the way to the Sweet 16 before losing to fellow mid-major Wichita State. The Explorers finished 3-2 in Big 5 play, earning their 11th Big 5 title. (Courtesy of the La Salle Athletic Department.)

This 2013 photograph shows the La Salle Explorers gathered on Selection Sunday awaiting their NCAA tournament fate. In program history, the Explorers have gone to 12 NCAA tournaments. They won in 1954, finished runner-up in 1955, made the Sweet 16 in 2013, the second round in 1983 and 1990, and lost in the first round in 1968, 1975, 1978, 1980, 1988, 1989, and 1992. The Explorers have also made 12 NIT appearances, with a win in 1952 and a runner-up finish in 1987.

Shown here during the January 9, 2013, matchup between La Salle and Charlotte are point guard Tyrone Garland (No. 21) and center Stephen Zack, as they guard Charlotte guard Terrance Williams. Although the Explorers lost this game, they went on to the Sweet 16 and a Big 5 title for the season. Garland currently plays professionally in Iceland after a stint in Canada. Zack plays professionally in Bulgaria after time in Latvia. He won a Bulgarian league championship in 2017.

The NCAA tournament is known for its Cinderella stories and tales of upsets, and the 2013 Explorers provided plenty of those. Despite an uneven season that saw them beat three ranked teams while losing to sub-.500 squads like Central Connecticut, the Explorers came ready to play. After winning their play-in game, the team shocked fourth-seed Kansas State by a score of 63-61. They then knocked off Ole Miss before dropping out after a loss to eventual Final Four participant Wichita State.

This ticket stub is from the January 7, 2015, matchup between La Salle and the Minutemen of the University of Massachusetts. The game ended in heartbreak for the Explorers, as they fell 74-67 to their Atlantic 10 counterparts. Massachusetts improved to 8-7 with the win, while the Explorers fell to a mediocre 8-7. After taking a 34-32 halftime lead, the Minutemen outscored La Salle 37-33 in the second half to seal the victory. Cleon Roberts led the Explorers with 17 points and five rebounds.

MB09	SECT.	ROW	SEAT	PRICE	SECT.	
	W5	V	5	$0.00	W5	MB09
$0.00						01/18/15
	TOM GOLA ARENA				ROW	12:30 PM
V5	LA SALLE UNIVERSITY				V	
V	vs.				SEAT	
	George Washington				5	SEASON
0005 SEASON						
					PRICE	7459
B	Sat. Jan 10, 2015 12:30 PM				$0.00	

La Salle rebounded with an upset win three days later, on January 10, 2015, over Atlantic 10 rivals George Washington by a score of 63-50. La Salle used a 33-19 lead at the half, coupled with almost even play in the second, to drop the Colonials to 12-4, while the Explorers improved to 9-7 in preparation for their remaining two Big 5 games of the season. Jordan Price led the Explorers with a 20-point outburst.

This photograph shows the entire 2015–2016 La Salle Explorers women's basketball team. The season was a rough one for the Explorers, as they staggered to a 5-25 record, including a dismal 0-4 in Big 5 play. In fact, the only bright spot for the Explorers in the Big 5 was a 75-70 win over Saint Joseph's, a game that did not count in the Big 5 standings because it was the second matchup of the year for the conference foes. The Explorers lost 77-48 to Temple, 78-68 to Penn, 67-56 to Villanova, and 64-55 to the Hawks.

Two

THE UNIVERSITY OF PENNSYLVANIA QUAKERS

In 1966, I was recruited to Penn by head coach Dick Harter and his assistant Digger Phelps. I was a wide-eyed, impressionable 17 year old who chose Penn during my first Palestra visit, enticed by the coaches' recruiting pitch that promised Ivy League and Big 5 domination, culminating in an eventual NCAA championship.

Logically, their expectations were overly optimistic. Despite Penn having its share of good teams and players, the Big 5 had been dominated by great Saint Joseph's, Villanova, Temple, and La Salle teams during its first decade. Those schools' rollouts, a Palestra game staple, referenced the Big 5 as "the Big 4 and Penn." To think that Penn would surmount all of this was farfetched.

I never asked Harter or Phelps if they really believed their hype or if it was just the work of super salesmen. In truth, what the team achieved during my years at Penn made that question moot. My junior and senior years, 1969–1970 and 1970–1971, we were undefeated in both the Ivy League and Big 5. Our overall combined record was 53-3, and in 1971, Penn was ranked third in the nation before being upset by archrival Villanova in the NCAA Elite Eight.

I believe that the turning point for our future success took place on the night of January 15, 1969, when our underdog team took on nationally ranked Villanova. We were not perfect that night, but with three minutes left in the game, the score was tied 30-30. A play was designated for me to shoot, one we had worked on a million times in practice. When I launched a 25-foot jump shot, I had no doubt it was going in, and I watched it slowly nestle into the net as time expired.

That 32-30 win was the last time we ever felt we needed a gimmick to win. The following year, forwards Corky Calhoun and Bob Morse joined my backcourt mate Dave Wohl and myself and a talented cast of teammates, creating a squad we felt was as good as any team in the country. Our success kicked off an amazing decade for Penn basketball that led to a Final Four appearance in 1979.

But in the late 1970s and early 1980s, things changed.

A visionary named Dave Gavitt formed the Big East. A national cable sports station, ESPN, was created, which turned college basketball from a local, parochial televised competition to a national experience. The Big 5 schools felt they needed to play more games on their own campuses rather than have all Big 5 games played in the Palestra. The magic of Big 5 basketball, though still profound, started to wane.

The Big 5 still exists and recently celebrated its 60th anniversary. But to anyone who ever witnessed or participated in the aura, the pageantry, the electricity, and the personalities of those early decades, words alone cannot truly capture that experience.

—Steve Bilsky
Former player, coach, and athletic director at Penn, executive director of the Big 5 (BA, Penn, 1971)

As the oldest institution in the Big 5 (and one of the 10 oldest in the nation), the University of Pennsylvania has a history stretching back to before the founding of the nation. Founded by a traveling evangelist in 1740, the school spent several of its early years in Center City before being forced to uproot and move to its current location across the Schuylkill River in West Philadelphia, now known as University City. This view shows, in the foreground, College Hall, which serves as a home to admissions, university president Amy Guttmann, and the history department. In the background is Claudia Cohen Hall, home to the School of Arts and Sciences and the religious studies department.

Established in 1878, the Penn Dental School traces its history to the Philadelphia College of Dental Surgery, which was founded in 1852. As one of 12 graduate schools at the university, it serves as one of the earliest schools of dental medicine in the United States. Although it started in Claudia Cohen Hall, it moved to the building pictured here in 1879 and remains there to this day. Among its notable alumni are famed Wild West gunman Doc Holiday, who graduated in 1872 and was a known associate of the famed Earp law family.

26

Standing in front of Franklin Field, this statue portrays a travelling Ben Franklin. Franklin served as a founding father of both the United States and of the University of Pennsylvania, which came to fruition after merging with an evangelical school (founded in 1740) in 1749. Franklin also served as the sixth president of Pennsylvania, the US ambassador to Sweden, the US ambassador to France, and the first postmaster general. He also helped Thomas Jefferson draft the Declaration of Independence in Philadelphia, a document that he signed on July 4, 1776.

Three-time All–Big 5 player and former University of Pennsylvania basketball captain Dick Censits is pictured here in 1957. Censits is one of only six Quakers in history to average double digits in both points and rebounds over the course of his career, finishing with 1,220 points and 867 rebounds. He was a first-team All–Ivy League selection as a senior and was inducted into the Big 5 Hall of Fame in 1981. Today, Censits serves on the university's board of trustees. (Courtesy of the University of Pennsylvania Digital Archives.)

This photograph shows the 1963–1964 Pennsylvania Quakers basketball squad. The team finished with a 14-10 record, including a 10-4 record in the Ivy League, which was good enough for third place. The Quakers finished with a 1-3 record in Big 5 play, with their lone win coming on January 29, 1964, in a 66-51 triumph over St. Joseph's. The Quakers, 6-7 after this victory, would go 8-3 the rest of the way. (Courtesy of the University of Pennsylvania Digital Archives.)

All–Ivy League forward John Edgar Wideman, seen here during the 1963–1964 season, is better known for his exploits off the hardwood, as he became the second African American to win a Rhodes Scholarship, which he used to attend Oxford. After graduating from the world-renowned Iowa Writer's Workshop at the University of Iowa, Wideman went on to a distinguished academic career at Brown University, where he taught English, creative writing, and African American studies. He has also held teaching posts at Penn, the University of Wyoming, and UMass-Amherst. (Courtesy of the University of Pennsylvania Digital Archives.)

John Edgar Wideman is preparing to shoot free throws during the 1963–1964 season. Penn finished the season 1-3 in Big 5 play, losing to Temple 65-55, to La Salle 61-58, and to Villanova in a 72-48 blowout. Their lone Big 5 win was against Saint Joseph's, 66-51. (Courtesy of the University of Pennsylvania Digital Archives.)

The 1970–1971 season, while one of the most successful in Penn history, was filled with oddities. The Quakers started the season 28-0, with a Big 5 championship, before falling apart against Big 5 rivals Villanova, 90-47, in the Elite Eight. That game, however, would later be changed to a win, as Villanova was found to have used an ineligible player. Thus, Penn stands as one of two teams in history to go undefeated and not win a national championship.

Chuck Daly is not the only connection that Penn has to the 1989–1990 Detroit Pistons teams that won back-to-back NBA titles. The general manager for those teams was Jack McCloskey, who, in a coincidence, headed up the Penn men's team between 1956 and 1966. He would led the Quakers to their first Big 5 title before leaving the bench in Philadelphia to coach at Wake Forest. A former Quaker himself whose career was interrupted by his service in World War II, McCloskey earned the moniker "Trade Joe" as his shrewd moves led the Pistons to the NBA's pinnacle.

In a five-year span, Dick Harter both led the Quakers to Ivy League success and positioned himself for greater things. Harter won two Ivy League titles and lost only one regular season game in his last two years at the helm. This also included two Big 5 championships. Shown here being honored at Oregon, Harter found great success as the Ducks coach before moving on to a 27-year career as an NBA assistant. He died in 2012 at the age of 81.

This 1971–1972 schedule featured senior center Corky Calhoun on the cover. The season was a remarkable one for the Quakers, as they ran a 25-3 record all the way to the Elite Eight and a regional runner-up finish. The Quakers finished 13-1 in the Ivy League, taking home the Ivy League title. Most importantly, however, the Quakers had a 3-1 record in the Big 5, beating Saint Joseph's 77-64, Villanova 74-64, and La Salle 80-77. The Quakers finished the season ranked third in the nation, capping their finest season in the modern history of the program.

Chuck Daly is an icon among basketball coaches. He led the Detroit Pistons to back-to-back NBA titles in 1989 and 1990, as well as coaching the 1992 "Dream Team" to Olympic gold. His success, however, can be traced back to Penn, where in six seasons he led the Quakers to five Ivy League titles, four Big 5 titles, and the Elite Eight in 1972. A two-time inductee to the Naismith Memorial Basketball Hall of Fame, Daly died of cancer in 2009.

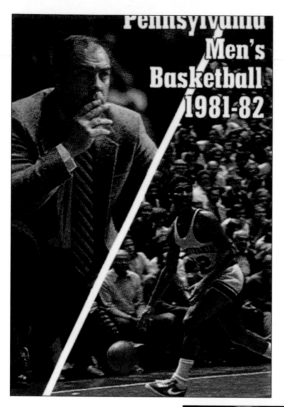

The 1981–1982 season was one of success for the Quakers. The team finished 17-10, which included a 12-2 record in Ivy League play, good enough for the Ivy League championship. The Quakers found less success in Big 5 play, finishing the round-robin with a 1-3 record. On December 12, 1981, the Quakers lost 75-61 to Villanova. That was followed by a 79-56 loss to Saint Joseph's on January 12 and a 77-75 loss to La Salle on January 19. The Quakers' lone Big 5 win that season came on February 9, with a 59-56 triumph over Temple. Featured on the front of this schedule are coach Bob Weinhauer and Ivy League Player of the Year Paul Little.

Shown here during his time at Arizona State is former Penn head coach Bob Weinhauer. A master of Ivy League basketball, Weinhauer won five Ivy League titles, compiling an incredible 62-9 record against his Ivy League opponents. While not quite as successful in the Big 5, he did manage to win two Big 5 titles in his stint at the helm of the Quakers. Weinhauer left the Quakers in 1982, having compiled a record of 99-45.

The 1982–1983 Quakers finished 17-9. It was good enough for second place in the Ivy League and improved their Big 5 record to 2-2, although Villanova claimed the Big 5 title for the season. Not all was lost in Big 5 lore for the Quakers, however, as they claimed an 84-80 victory over 10th-ranked Villanova on December 11, 1982, and a 78-72 win over La Salle on December 8, although losses to Saint Joseph's (85-79) and Temple (61-53) followed. Featured on the front of this card are co-captains Michael Brown (left) and Paul Little, who was the prior season's Ivy League Player of the Year.

The 1983–1984 Quakers faced a significant drop-off as they stumbled to at 10-16 record, which included 7-7 and fourth place in the Ivy League. The Quakers also finished 0-4 in Big 5 play. On January 14, 1984, they fell to Saint Joseph's 86-66. This was followed by a January 24 loss to La Salle, 96-85. Up next was an 81-57 drubbing at the hands of Temple, part of a six-game losing streak. The Quakers finished with a 65-51 loss to Villanova on February 21. Featured on the front of this card is guard Anthony Arnolie, who averaged 10.5 points per contest for the Quakers.

Craig Littlepage was a star player at Penn from 1970 to 1973, winning a Big 5 championship in each of his three years as a player. After graduating from the Wharton School in 1973, Littlepage spent several years as an assistant (including at Big 5 rival Villanova) before taking the Penn head coaching job in 1982. His success as a player was not replicated as a coach, and after stints at Rutgers and Virginia, he took the position of athletic director at the latter.

Mike Jordan, a four-year starter for the Quakers, helped lead Penn to back-to-back Ivy League titles in 1999 and 2000, although he was never a part of a Big 5 championship team. Jordan's accomplishments, however, cannot be understated, as he graduated with 1,604 points, the fourth-highest total in Quaker history. Jordan followed his time at Penn with a stellar career in Europe, playing in Germany, Spain, Italy, Latvia, Belgium, Greece, and Israel.

The 2003–2004 season was a decent one for the Quakers, as they finished 17-10, including 10-4 in the Ivy League, good for second place. The Quakers, however, would stumble to a 1-3 record in Big 5 play. On December 6, they lost to 12th-ranked (and eventual Big 5 champions) Saint Joseph's by a tally of 67-59. Three days later, the Quakers fell to the Villanova Wildcats 73-63. On January 14, the Quakers demolished the La Salle Explorers 71-47. Finally, the Quakers lost to the Temple Owls 73-69 on January 21. On the front of this schedule is senior Adam Chubb, who averaged 10.5 points and 7.5 rebounds.

UNIVERSITY OF PENNSYLVANIA
2003-04 MEN'S BASKETBALL

Senior
Adam Chubb

Nov. 21	WISCONSIN	6 p.m.
Nov. 24	DREXEL	8 p.m.
Nov. 29	at Michigan State*	2 p.m.
Nov. 30	DePaul/Indiana State*	2/4 p.m.
Dec. 6	SAINT JOSEPH'S&	2:30 p.m.
Dec. 9	VILLANOVA	8 p.m.
Dec. 20	at Bucknell	3 p.m.
Dec. 28	St. John's#	4 p.m.
Dec. 29	Manhattan/Holy Cross#	7/9 p.m.
Jan. 7	LAFAYETTE	7 p.m.
Jan. 10	at Rider	7:30 p.m.
Jan. 14	at La Salle	4 p.m.
Jan. 21	TEMPLE	8 p.m.
Jan. 30	at Yale	8 p.m.
Jan. 31	at Brown	7 p.m.
Feb. 6	HARVARD	7 p.m.
Feb. 7	DARTMOUTH	7 p.m.
Feb. 10	at Princeton	8 p.m.
Feb. 13	at Columbia	7 p.m.
Feb. 14	at Cornell	8 p.m.
Feb. 20	BROWN	7 p.m.
Feb. 21	YALE	8 p.m.
Feb. 27	CORNELL	7 p.m.
Feb. 28	COLUMBIA	7 p.m.
Mar. 5	at Dartmouth	7 p.m.
Mar. 6	at Harvard	7 p.m.
Mar. 9	PRINCETON	7 p.m.

ALL DATES AND TIMES ARE SUBJECT TO CHANGE.
* Coca Cola Classic, East Lansing, Mich.
& Big 5 Classic, The Palestra
# Holiday Classic, Madison Sq. Garden

www.pennathletics.com
Tickets: 215-898-6151

As the only coach to ever head up two Big 5 programs, Fran Dunphy has a unique perspective into Big 5 basketball. The fact that he played for La Salle in his collegiate days makes that perspective even more amazing. After winning one Big 5 title as a player, Dunphy coached Penn to four Big 5 titles before leaving the Quakers to replace John Chaney at Temple in 2006. He has since led the Owls to four more Big 5 titles. He has more wins than any other coach for a Big 5 team and has earned the moniker "Mr. Big 5."

Shown in front of his bench is former Quakers coach Glen Miller, currently an assistant at the University of Connecticut. Miller's tenure at Penn was a rough one; after compiling a 93-99 record at Brown, he surprised a lot of people in the college basketball community when he led the Quakers to a 22-9 record in his first season, capped off by an NCAA tournament appearance. His remaining time at Penn was far less successful, and he was fired after an 0-7 start to the 2009–2010 season. The Quakers won no Big 5 titles under his watch.

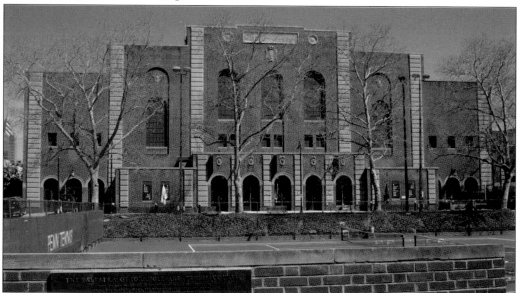

The Palestra, Penn's 10,000-seat basketball arena, was constructed in 1926 and opened on January 1, 1927. The initial aim of the Big 5 was to pay for upkeep for the ancient arena, and it was not uncommon for the teams to play double- or even triple-headers there. The Palestra has hosted more games, visiting teams, and NCAA tournament games than any other arena in the history of college basketball. Today, it plays host to some Big 5 games and to the Ivy League tournament.

Justin Reilly (No. 41) prepares for his last game at the Palestra in 2010. While part of a heralded recruiting class, injuries kept Reilly from realizing his full potential, although as a freshman he played a huge role in Penn winning the Ivy League championship. After making the tournament, Reilly buried three huge three pointers in a game that saw Penn nearly upset Texas A&M in the first round. Reilly graduated from the Wharton School at Penn in 2010.

Shown here with coach Jerome Allen is Zack Rosen, one of Penn's most recent All-Americans. A Quaker from 2008 to 2012, Rosen is Penn's all-time leader in assists, minutes, and games started and is third overall in scoring. A three-time All–Ivy League selection, Rosen was Big 5 Rookie of the Year in 2009, an All-American in 2012, and the winner of the Robert V. Geasey trophy in 2012. After going unselected in the NBA draft, Rosen made his way to Israel, where he continues to play professionally.

Former Penn coach Jerome Allen is currently an assistant coach for the Boston Celtics. After a four-year career at Penn, which saw him win two Big 5 titles, Allen was the 49th overall pick in the 1995 NBA draft. After stints with the Timberwolves, Nuggets, and Pacers, Allen spent the rest of his career playing in Turkey, Greece, Spain, France, and Italy. He compiled a 65-104 record at Penn.

Shown here are the Penn Quakers in their Big 5 matchup against La Salle on November 29, 2014. Penn handed La Salle a tough 57-29 defeat en route to a 3-1 Big 5 record and a share of the Big 5 championship. After finishing runner-up in the Ivy League, the Quakers made the second round of the women's NIT, winning a first-round matchup against Hofstra University before losing a rematch to Big 5 rival Temple in the second round.

Miles Jackson-Cartwright was a four-year member of the Quakers basketball team. The highest-ranked recruit to ever commit to Penn, Jackson-Cartwright had a successful stint as a Quaker, where he was a three-time team captain and an All–Ivy League honoree in 2013. He also won the Big 5 Cy Kaselman Award for best free throw shooting percentage in 2013. Jackson-Cartwright currently plays in Europe, having played for teams in the Netherlands and Germany.

Shown here is the November 25, 2015, matchup between Big 5 rivals Penn and La Salle at the Palestra. In what would amount to a horrid 11-17 season, this game was one of the few bright spots for the Quakers, who defeated the Explorers 80-64. That was the only Big 5 win for the Quakers that season, as they were blown out by Saint Joseph's and Villanova and lost a heartbreaker to Temple.

This interior view of the Palestra shows Big 5 rivals Penn and Saint Joseph's warming up about 30 minutes prior to their clash on January 28, 2016. The Hawks took the matchup by a tally of 47-44, but not all was lost for the Quakers. Despite a 1-3 run in the Big 5, Penn finished the season 20-8, with an Ivy League championship to their credit. This was good enough to earn the Quakers a 15 seed in the NCAA tournament, where they fell to second seed Texas (and future NBA stars LaMarcus Aldridge and P.J. Tucker) by a score of 60-52.

Pictured are the back-to-back Ivy League champions from the Quakers women's team. In 2015–2016, despite a 2-2 record in the Big 5, the Quakers finished the season 24-5, including an Ivy League title and a 10 seed in the NCAA tournament, where they fell to Washington. Despite an 0-4 record in the Big 5 in 2016–2017, the Lady Quakers finished 22-8, capping their season with a second Ivy League title and an NCAA tournament berth, where they lost to five seed Texas A&M.

This image shows a matchup between Penn and second-ranked Villanova at the Palestra on November 29, 2016. Fresh off its NCAA championship run, Villanova was in no mood to show pity for their Big 5 rivals, as the Wildcats thrashed the Quakers 82-57. For the season, the Quakers finished 13-15, with a meager 1-3 record in Big 5 play. Their only win was at La Salle on January 25, when they outscored the Explorers 77-74.

With the beautiful skyline of Philadelphia as a backdrop, Franklin Field is seen here along with the longtime home of the Philadelphia Big 5, the Palestra. The Palestra is considered the birthplace of college basketball and is also home to the Battle of 33rd Street, an annual matchup between Penn and Drexel, during alternating seasons.

Shown here is current Quakers head coach Steve Donahue. A four-year starter at Ursinus College, Donahue was an assistant coach at Penn from 1990 to 2000 before taking the head coaching job at rival Cornell. After three straight NCAA berths (including a Sweet 16 run in 2010), Donahue took the coaching job at Boston College. Four years later, he took over at Penn, where his record stood at 24-31 entering the 2017–2018 season.

Three

THE SAINT JOSEPH'S UNIVERSITY HAWKS

One of a kind . . . unique . . . has not been duplicated.

The athletic directors of five Greater Philadelphia institutions of higher learning gathered to discuss combining forces in showcasing men's college basketball. At the time, these institutions were playing in two separate venues: Penn and Villanova at the Palestra, and Temple, La Salle, and Saint Joseph's at Convention Hall, a mere two blocks from the Palestra.

The question quickly became, "Why can't all play at the Palestra in a doubleheader format?" Bingo! Thus, the Philadelphia Big 5 was born.

The first season of play was 1955–1956, and it was an immediate hit among the fans in Philadelphia. The concept involved one Big 5 school playing another (which they had not done previously) and sharing the other half of a doubleheader, where one of the other schools played an out-of-area competitor.

While many format changes would take place over the next 60 years, there was one constant: The schools continued to play each other. A women's round-robin competition began in the 1980s.

Above all else, however, the Big 5 is the people who played and coached the game: Rodgers, Lear, Ramsay, Anderson, Jones, Litwack, Guokas, White, Wideman, Corace, McCloskey, Kraft, Durrett, Porter, Bilsly, Wohl, and countless others in the first 15 years. Many former players and coaches went on to legendary NBA careers as well.

Saturday nights at the Palestra were magic, special, and memorable for hundreds of thousands of fans over the years. The major development of conference play and the importance of qualifying for the NCAA tournament may have taken some of the "specialness" away, but the rivalries continue to this day. May that always be the case!

—Dominick DiJulia
Former player and athletic director, Saint Joseph's (BA, Saint Joseph's, 1967)

Naismith Memorial Basketball Hall of Fame coach Jack Ramsay was a legend in Philadelphia coaching circles. Dr. Ramsay served as the Hawks coach for 10 seasons, leading the team to seven of its 20 Big 5 titles, including five solo titles, all with a 4-0 record. On doctor's advice, he retired in 1966, only to take the general manager's job with the Philadelphia 76ers. Under his guidance, the team finished 68-13, winning the NBA title. In short order, Ramsay returned to the coaching bench, coaching the 76ers, Braves, Trail Blazers (whom he led to a 1977 NBA title), and Pacers. Later in life, he provided television coverage for the 76ers, Heat, and ESPN. Coach Ramsay died of cancer in 2014 at the age of 89.

Saint Joseph's Hawks legend Bob McNeil goes up against NBA Hall of Famer Bill Russell in a regular season NBA game in 1962. While with the Hawks, McNeil set the record for most assists in a season, in a game, and average for a career, the last of which still stands today. In the three seasons that McNeil started for the Hawks, the team won two Big 5 championships, and McNeil was named All–Big 5 each season. An All-American his senior season, he led the Hawks to a 60-21 record over his three years and was elected to the Big 5 Hall of Fame in 1974.

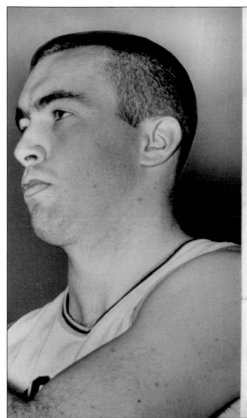

The legacy of the 1960–1961 Saint Joseph's Hawks basketball team is a strange one, clouded in controversy and success. The team initially finished its season 25-5, with a third-place finish in the NCAA tournament. However, shown here are Jack Egan (left) and Vince Kempton, who were expelled from Saint Joseph's on April 24 after being indicted by New York district attorney Frank Hogan on charges that they accepted bribes to fix basketball games. The school forfeited three games, and lost mention of a loss against La Salle, another team embroiled in the scandal. The Hawks won the Big 5 for the season with a 4-0 mark.

Former Saint Joseph's swingman Matt Guokas Jr. Guokas, along with being one of the Hawks all-time leaders in both steals and assists, is part of the first father-son duo to win an NBA championship; his father won the 1946 title with the Philadelphia Warriors, and he won with the Philadelphia 76ers in 1967. After being drafted ninth overall by the 76ers, Guokas went on to a 10-year NBA career, playing for the 76ers, Bulls, Royals, Rockets, Braves, and Kings before retiring in 1976. He later found success as a coach with the 76ers and the Magic. His son Matt III later played for the Hawks as well.

Center Chuck McKenna grabs a rebound against two players from Xavier University during the 1964–1965 season. This season was one of wild success for the Hawks, who finished the year with a 26-3 record, including an undefeated 4-0 en route to the Big 5 championship. They won each of their Big 5 games by a margin of at least eight points. As for this game, the Hawks took a 93-78 win over Xavier at the old Cincinnati Gardens. Malcolm W. Emmons took the photograph.

This photograph shows the opening tip for a Big 5 matchup between the Saint Joseph's Hawks and the University of Pennsylvania Quakers at the Palestra during the 1965–1966 season. The Hawks won this game 79-69 en route to a 24-5 record, including an undefeated 4-0 in the Big 5, leading to the school's seventh Big 5 championship. The Hawks capped their season with a top five national ranking. (Courtesy of the University of Pennsylvania Digital Archives.)

Although Mike Bantom was never part of one of the Hawk's Big 5 championship teams, he is still a legend in the history of both Saint Joseph's and the Big 5. Bantom, a two-time All–Big 5 selection, was the number two rebounder in Hawks history (1,151) and was sixth in total points scored (1,684). In his three seasons, he averaged a double-double, and led the Hawks in scoring twice and rebounds three times. Bantom left school as a junior and spent 10 seasons in the NBA, averaging 12.1 points and 6.4 rebounds. He also earned a silver medal as a member of the 1972 US men's team at the Munich Olympics, although it was never received, in protest.

The December 13, 1972, game between Saint Joseph's and Penn at the Palestra was the Big 5 kickoff of the season for both squads. Penn won a thriller, 54-53, on its way to a 21-6 season, a national ranking of 18, and an Ivy League title, all in addition to its perfect 4-0 Big 5 championship. For their part, the Hawks finished 22-6, with a 3-2 record in Big 5 play (with two wins in back-to-back games against La Salle). The Hawks also won the Mid-Atlantic Conference before bowing out in the first round of the NCAA tournament. (Courtesy of the University of Pennsylvania Digital Archives.)

47

In his three-year tenure as Hawks head coach, Jim Lynam led his squads to two Big 5 titles, although the second (part of the first five-way tie in Big 5 history) was a memorable one. Unranked, the Hawks entered the NCAA tournament as a nine seed, knocking off Creighton before upsetting DePaul, the No. 1 team in the nation at the time. The Hawks made their way to the Elite Eight, where they fell to eventual national champion Indiana. After NBA coaching stops with the Clippers, 76ers, and Bullets, Lynam took a role in the Timberwolves front office before joining on-air coverage for the 76ers.

The front of this 1982–1983 schedule shows Saint Joseph's center Tony Costner. Although Saint Joseph's was unable to duplicate its success of the prior year (losing both the Big 5 championship and failing to make the NCAA tournament), Costner had a stellar year, averaging 15.2 points and 9.4 rebounds per contest. Costner was an honorable mention All-American in 1983 and was inducted into the Big 5 Hall of Fame in 1990. The Hawks were 2-2 in Big 5 play that season, beating Penn and La Salle but losing to Temple and eventual champions Villanova.

This press photograph shows former Saint Joseph's head coach Jim Boyle. The caption reads, "The head coach of Saint Joseph's in Philadelphia Jim Boyle fields questions Saturday morning as he discusses his team's advancement into second-round action on Sunday at the Syracuse Carrier Dome. Photo by Richard T. Conway." The Hawks lost that 1986 second-round game to Cleveland State by a score of 75-69. Saint Joseph's finished the year 26-6, with an Atlantic 10 and Big 5 title.

After spending four years at Saint Joseph's (and winning a Big 5 title in 1985–1986), former Hawks star and current Rider head coach Kevin Baggett embarked on a coaching career that saw him spend time as an assistant at Western Kentucky, Howard, Coastal Carolina, the University of Maryland at Baltimore County, and Rider before taking the head coaching gig in 2012. In five years, Baggett has an 85-78 record and two postseason appearances in minor, one-off tournaments.

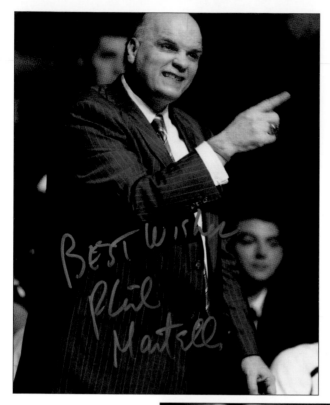

This autographed picture shows Saint Joseph's coaching legend Phil Martelli, currently in his 22nd season as the head coach of the Hawks. Martelli sported a 414-293 record at the end of the 2016–2017 season. The Hawks made seven NCAA tournament appearances under Martelli, including an Elite Eight appearance in 2003–2004, a season when the Hawks started 27-0. In addition to six NIT appearances (two of which resulted in runner-up finishes), the Hawks have won four Big 5 championships under Martelli's watch. Six Hawks have made it to the NBA under Martelli's stewardship, including Jameer Nelson, who was an NBA All-Star in 2009.

James "Bruiser" Flint is a member of the Saint Joseph's Hawks Basketball Hall of Fame. A four-year letter winner, Flint was named to the All–Atlantic 10 team his senior season and was inducted into the hall of fame in 1988. A Philadelphia native, he returned home to coach City 6 rival Drexel for 15 seasons, where he won a conference championship and four conference Coach of the Year awards. Today, Flint is an assistant coach at Indiana.

Shown on the front of this schedule is Mike Shaak, a four-year letter winner for the Hawks. In 1989–1990 (his senior season), he was named co-captain for a Hawks squad that went a miserable 7-21, including a dismal 1-3 in Big 5 play. For his career, Shaak averaged 5.6 points, 3.3 rebounds, and half an assist per contest. The Hawks came up short in the Big 5 in each of his seasons, as La Salle dominated the conference.

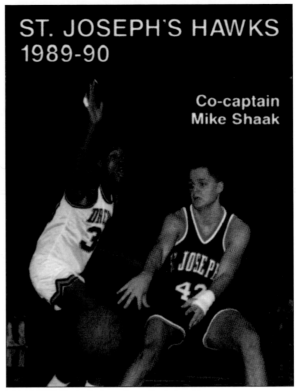

ST. JOSEPH'S HAWKS 1989-90

Co-captain Mike Shaak

ST. JOSEPH'S UNIVERSITY HAWKS

1995 SPRING SPORTS SCHEDULE
Baseball

Big 5 competition is not limited to basketball. This is the 1995 spring baseball schedule for Saint Joseph's, which, much in the Philadelphia tradition, managed to squeeze in each of the other Big 5 schools for at least one game. This season was a mediocre one for the Hawks, as they finished 12-12 in Atlantic 10 play and 25-30 overall, failing to qualify for the College World Series. Danny Lauer led the team with a .373 batting average, and Jed Johnson pitched his way to an 8-6 record. Two-way star Bill Weingarter hit .359 and recorded four wins on the mound.

Coach John Gallagher has a long, winding tradition with the Big 5, which started with his career as a Hawk from 1996 to 1999. After winning one Big 5 title, Gallagher graduated and joined the coaching ranks, starting as an assistant at Big 5 rival La Salle. He also had assistant gigs at Lafayette, Hartford, and Big 5 rival Penn before taking the head coaching job at Hartford, where he has compiled a 94-140 record, along with a postseason berth in 2013.

Saint Joseph's legend Jameer Nelson was a four-year starter for the Hawks. Named the 2004 National Collegiate Player of the year, he was also a first-team All-American, a three-time All–Atlantic 10 selection, and a two-time All–Atlantic 10 all-defensive team selection. The Hawks finished 30-2 in Nelson's senior year, coming within a last-second shot of the Final Four. In addition, the Hawks won the Big 5 twice under Nelson's guidance, each time with a 4-0 record. Nelson was named to the Big 5 Hall of Fame in 2017. A first-round draft choice in 2004 by the Orlando Magic, he is still playing in the NBA. He made the NBA All-Star team in 2009 and led the Magic to the NBA finals.

Jameer Nelson's backcourt partner was Delonte West, a successful player in his own right. In addition to being a third-team All-American, West was twice named to the All–Atlantic 10 team. The Hawks won two Big 5 titles during his tenure. After his junior season, he declared for the NBA draft, where the Boston Celtics took him in the first round. After stints with Boston, Seattle, Cleveland, Minnesota, and Dallas, West played for two separate Chinese pro teams before retiring, due to injuries, after the 2015 season. The 2003–2004 Hawks team led by Nelson and West was inducted into the Big 5 Hall of Fame in 2015.

Shown here playing in France is former Saint Joseph's power forward Ahmad Nivins. The 2009 season was a memorable one for Nivins, as he took home All-American and All–Atlantic 10 honors and was named both the Atlantic 10 and Big 5 Player of the Year. After being drafted in the second round of the 2009 NBA draft by the Dallas Mavericks, Nivins played in Spain, Belgium, and France, where he was a French Pro A All-Star in 2012.

Shown here playing stout defense is former Saint Joseph's Hawks and current National Basketball League (NBL) of Canada All-Star Garrett Williamson (left). Although Williamson never won a Big 5 title as a Hawk, he did have a successful career. In 2009 and 2010, he was named to the All–Atlantic 10 defensive team. After going undrafted in the 2010 NBA draft, Williamson played for both Tulsa and Austin as well as for professional teams in Germany, Greece, and Canada, where he was the 2014 NBL MVP.

Although Saint Joseph's, at 20-14, failed to make the NCAA tournament for the 2011–2012 season (instead falling in the first round of the NIT), they did manage to claim a share of the Big 5 title for that season with Temple, at 3-1. Shown on the front of this schedule is Langston Galloway, who averaged 15.5 points, 4.5 rebounds, and 2.2 assists en route to a second-team All–Atlantic 10 selection. Galloway currently plays for the NBA's Sacramento Kings, where he was traded by the New Orleans Pelicans on February 20, 2017. While playing for the New York Knicks in 2015, he was named to the NBA All-Rookie Second Team.

The men's teams are not the only ones that participate in Big 5 play. The women's teams for each school hold a Big 5 classic of their own. This is the schedule for the 2011–2012 Saint Joseph's women, who finished 22-11 and advanced to the second round of the WNIT. The Lady Hawks finished 2-3 in Big 5 play for the season, with wins over Penn and La Salle and losses to Villanova and Temple (twice). Michelle Baker is featured on the front of this card. Baker is the all-time leader in games played for the Lady Hawks and averaged 12.2 points per contest in 2011–2012. She currently serves as an assistant coach at Drexel.

Featured in this autographed photograph is former Saint Joseph's Hawk and current Detroit Piston Langston Galloway. Galloway was with the Hawks from 2010 to 2014, where he won a Big 5 title in 2011–2012 and left as the second-highest scorer in Hawks history, behind Jameer Nelson. Although undrafted in the 2014 NBA draft, Galloway signed with the New York Knicks, where he was NBA All-Rookie Second Team in 2015. After leaving the Knicks, he signed with the New Orleans Pelicans before being traded to the Sacramento Kings. After the 2016–2017 season, he signed with the Pistons.

Halil Kanacevic is just one of many players to represent his country, Montenegro, in international play after playing in the Big 5. After his freshman season at Hofstra University, Kanacevic transferred to Saint Joseph's, where he was a part of the 2011–2012 Big 5 championship squad. Undrafted by the NBA, Kanacevic has taken his game to the international pros, playing in Italy, Slovenia, Israel, Spain, and Montenegro.

The Hawks won this February 4, 2012, matchup against La Salle 70-66 on the way to their 20th Big 5 title. Halil Kanacevic put up 18 points and grabbed 15 rebounds for Saint Joseph's, while Earl Pettis put up 17 points for the Explorers. For the season, the finished 20-14, with a loss in the first round of the NIT. They shared the Big 5 title with Temple.

This action shot was taken during the February 2, 2013, showdown between Saint Joseph's and Temple. Although Temple would go on to take the Big 5 title for the season (an honor it shared with La Salle), this day belonged to the Hawks in a 70-69 thriller. Ronald Roberts led the way with 18 points, 12 rebounds, and 3 blocked shots. C.J. Aiken and Carl Jones each added 16 points to the Hawks' upset effort.

Ronald Roberts was a four-year letter winner for the Saint Joseph's Hawks and led the team to a 2011–2012 Big 5 title. In his four-year career, he received the Robert O'Neil Memorial trophy as the Hawks' most improved player, the Atlantic 10 Sixth Man of the Year award, and two third-team All–Atlantic 10 honors. After going undrafted in the 2014 NBA draft, Roberts spent time in the NBA D-League and played for professional teams in the Philippines, Turkey, and Israel.

C.J. Aiken, a three-year letter winner for the Hawks from 2010 to 2013, was one of the top shot blockers in the nation, which helped lead the Hawks to the 2011–2012 Big 5 title. Aiken was the Atlantic 10 Defensive Player of the Year and made the Atlantic 10 All-Defensive team. He was undrafted in the 2013 NBA draft, although his professional career has seen him play in the NBA G League and in Poland and Canada.

Former Hawks star Carl Jones played for Saint Joseph's from 2009 to 2013. He enjoyed moderate success as a Hawk, including helping his team win the 2011–2012 Big 5 championship. After going undrafted in the 2013 NBA draft, Jones played professionally for teams in Macedonia, Kosovo, and Mexico, where today he plays for Mineros des Zacatecas.

Former Saint Joseph's forward DeAndre' Bembry last played for the Hawks in the 2015–2016 season. A six-foot, six-inch talent with impeccable ball-handling skills and a deadly jumper, Bembry was twice named to the first-team All–Atlantic 10 squad and was an honorable mention for All-American honors. His talent led to him being a first-round draft choice of the Atlanta Hawks (21st overall), where he is expected to play a huge role in Atlanta's rebuilding youth movement.

One of DeAndre' Bembry's running mates was Isaiah Miles, a four-year letter winner for the Hawks. Although Miles never won a Big 5 title, he did enjoy success as a Hawk, earning most improved player honors in both the Atlantic 10 and the Big 5 during his senior season. He led the Hawks in points per game (18.1), rebounding (8.1) and blocks (1.0). Undrafted in the 2016 NBA draft, Miles went abroad, where he plays for Usaf Sportif in the Turkish Premier League.

Hagan Arena is home to the Saint Joseph's Hawks. Originally constructed in 1949, it spent the early part of its life known as Alumni Fieldhouse. In 2009, while coupled with the Hawks' rise to national prominence and the newer arenas at Temple and La Salle, the building underwent a $25 million renovation. The building is named after Michael Hagan, an alum who donated $10 million to the renovation project. Today, aside from basketball, it hosts a series of concerts, squash courts, faculty offices, and student locker rooms.

Four

THE TEMPLE UNIVERSITY OWLS

College basketball started at Temple University in 1894, just three years after Dr. James Naismith invented the game. Temple basketball is the fifth winningest program in Division One, just behind the powerhouse programs of Kentucky, Kansas, North Carolina, and Duke. Since the formation of the Big 5 in 1955, Temple has the most Big 5 championships, at 27.

Temple has produced many great coaches, most notably Harry Litwack and John Chaney. Both have been elected to the Naismith Memorial Basketball Hall of Fame. Temple also lays claim to Guy Rodgers, a record-setting ball handler who was elected to the Naismith Memorial Basketball Hall of Fame in 2014. To date, he is the only Owl to receive this honor.

On a national scale, Temple has won two national championships: the 1938 NIT and the 1969 NIT. Harry Litwack coached the 1969 champions; following the game, he said it was "the happiest day" of his coaching career. It was an honor to have been a part of that team. Temple was the last team picked for the field. However, we moved on to win four games, with an unexpected victory over Boston College in the nationally televised finals played at Madison Square Garden. Boston College, coached by Hall of Famer Bob Cousy, had won 19 consecutive games before their loss to us.

Temple basketball has also reached the Final Four twice, both times coached by Harry Litwack. Coach John Chaney created a special team in 1988, and it was ranked No. 1 in all the national polls for most of the season. The Owls finished the season with a 32-2 record, and John Chaney was selected National Coach of the Year.

Temple has produced a wide assortment of players going into the NBA. I was fortunate to be one of those players. I was drafted in the second round of the NBA draft in 1969 by the Chicago Bulls as the 22nd overall pick. Graduating from Temple University with my class in 1969 and playing in the fabled Palestra were two of the highlights of my life.

—John Baum
Big 5 Hall of Famer and current Temple Radio color commentator (BS, Temple, 1969)

(Author's note: John "Jumpin' Johnny" Baum played for Temple from 1966 to 1969. Despite not having played in high school, he went on to great success and is a member of the Big 5, Temple, and MAC Halls of Fame.)

Temple University was founded as a private institution in 1884 by Baptist minister Russell Conwell. As illustrated by the banner on this postcard, the school's colors are cherry and white, which can often be found trimmed in gold. Temple's first basketball season was in 1894, when the team played to an 8-3 record. Temple won its first and only national championship in 1938, winning the NIT in the last year before the NCAA tournament was established.

Conwell Hall and Carnell Hall are the main academic and administrative buildings at Temple. Conwell Hall is the building at right. It houses administrative offices and classrooms as well as a swimming pool. The taller building at left is Carnell Hall, which also has classrooms and administrative offices. There is also a post office and student store in this building.

This photograph shows the interior of the Sol Feinstone Student Center at Temple. The women's basketball team at Temple also participates in the Big 5, with championships in 1983, 1986, 2002, 2005–2009, and 2011. The team has made 10 appearances in the NCAA tournament and six appearances in the WNIT.

This photograph shows Temple standout and Naismith Memorial Basketball Hall of Famer Guy Rodgers. Out of Philadelphia's Northeast High School, Rodgers spent three seasons with the Owls, claiming three Big 5 titles. Drafted by the Philadelphia Warriors in the 1958 NBA draft, Rodgers teamed with fellow Hall of Famer Wilt Chamberlin to lead the Warriors to several playoff appearances. Rodgers was a four-time NBA All-Star, a two-time NBA leader in assists, and was twice named an All-American. He was posthumously inducted into the Hall of Fame in 2014. (Courtesy of the University of Pennsylvania Digital Archives.)

Temple Hall of Famer Bill Kennedy is a rarity amongst Robert V. Geasey Trophy winners in that his squad did not win the Big 5 in the year that he won the award. The 1959–1960 season saw a tie between Saint Joseph's and Villanova for the title, the first for the Wildcats. Temple finished 1-3 in the Big 5, 17-9 overall, and lost in the first round of the NIT. Kennedy played seven games for the Philadelphia Warriors before retiring. He died in a Florida car crash in 2006. (Courtesy of the Temple Athletic Department.)

Big 5 Hall of Famer and 1961 Robert V. Geasey Trophy winner Bruce Drysdale was a three-time letter winner for the Owls and made the All–Big 5 team during his junior and senior seasons. The Owls were unable to capitalize on Drysdale's individual success, as the team failed to win the Big 5 in any of his seasons. For his career, Drysdale scored 1,444 points. Not just limited to the hardwood, Drysdale was a three-year varsity golfer for the Owls as well. After his playing days, he graduated from the Temple School of Dentistry and went into private practice. (Courtesy of the Temple Athletic Department.)

Johnny Baum is a legend among Temple fans. A three-year starter for the Owls, Baum's teams were frustrated in their pursuit of a Big 5 title, going 3-1 in 1966–1967 (Villanova went 4-0), 2-2 in 1967–1968 (Saint Joseph's went 3-1), and 2-2 in 1968–1969 (La Salle went 4-0). However, the Owls had greater national success, winning the NIT in 1968 and making the postseason in each of Baum's three years. He was the first Owl to record both 1,000 career points and 1,000 career rebounds. Baum was elected to the Big 5 Hall of Fame in 1978. (Courtesy of the Temple Athletic Department.)

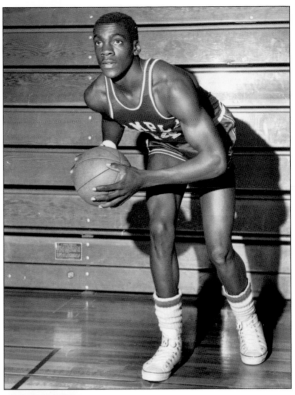

Baum's ties to Temple did not end with his playing days. After a two-year stint with the Chicago Bulls, he jumped to the ABA and played a combined 244 games for the New Jersey Nets, Memphis Tams, Indiana Pacers, Hazelton Bullets, and Allentown Jets. The Nets and Pacers later joined the NBA. After his playing career, Baum spent several years in banking and finance (turning down a chance to join the San Antonio Spurs at one point) before returning home to do color commentary for the Owls, a post that he mans to this day. Always a delight to work with, his contributions to this volume are many and varied. (Courtesy of the Temple Athletic Department.)

Featured here is 1979 Robert V. Geasey Trophy winner Ricky Reed. Reed was a four-year letterman for the Owls, leaving with career averages of 9.4 points and 7.2 assists. His senior year was the high-water mark of his career, as he averaged 15.7 points and 7.2 assists per game. Temple shared three Big 5 titles in Reed's four years there, including a 3-1 mark in the 1978–1979 season, equaled by Penn. The Quakers, however, owned the season victory over the Owls with a 79-74 barn burner at the Palestra. Temple finished the season with a 24-4 record and an NCAA tournament berth. (Courtesy of the Temple Athletic Department.)

This schedule covered all winter sports for the 1981–1982 season. In men's basketball, the Owls posted a 19-8 record, winning the East Coast Conference with an 11-0 record in conference play (although they fell in the first round of both the league tournament and the NIT) and the Big 5 with a 3-1 record, a title they shared with Saint Joseph's. The Owls' only Big 5 loss of the season was at the hands of Penn, 59-56, on February 9, 1982.

Temple University Winter Sports Schedule 1981 — 1982

Department of Men's Intercollegiate Athletics

Director—Ernest C. Casale
Associate Director—Gavin White
Assistant Director—Al Shrier
Assistant Director—Frank Walker
Business Manager—Neil Bress

Naismith Memorial Basketball Hall of Fame coach John Chaney, who is also a member of the Big 5 Hall of Fame, took Temple to the Elite Eight five times during his tenure and entered the 1987–1988 tournament as the No. 1 team in the nation. The Owls won a staggering 15 Big 5 titles under his guidance. Known as a fierce competitor and a loyal steward of his players (who he guided with a firm hand), Cheney will be most remembered for making Temple a national contender year in and year out.

Pictured here is 1983 Robert V. Geasey Trophy co-recipient and former Temple Owl Terrence Stansbury. Stansbury starred for the Owls between 1980 and 1984, where he earned Atlantic 10 Player of the Year (1984) and third-team All-American (1984) honors. Temple won three Big 5 titles in his time, with the only non-championship season being the one in which he won the Robert V. Geasey Trophy. Stansbury went on to have a three-year NBA career, each year taking third place in the NBA Slam Dunk competition. His daughter Tiffany spent three seasons in the WNBA. (Courtesy of the Temple Athletic Department.)

Nate Blackwell, 1987 Robert V. Geasey Trophy winner, played for the Owls from 1983 to 1987, during which time Temple won three Big 5 titles, including one in the 1987 season. During that season, Blackwell was also named Atlantic 10 Player of the Year and third-team All-American. A second-round pick of the San Antonio Spurs, Blackwell spent 10 games with the team in 1987. He has the distinction of being coach John Chaney's first Temple recruit. A member of the Temple Hall of Fame, Blackwell returned to the Owls as an assistant coach in 1996. (Courtesy of the Temple Athletic Department.)

Robert V Geasey Trophy winner Mark Macon was a four-year letterman for the Owls, while taking part in three Big 5 championship teams. After three years in La Salle legend Lionel Simmons's shadow, Macon was able to add the Robert V. Geasey Trophy to a list of accolades that include Atlantic 10 Player of the Year (1989), second-team All-American (1991), and NBA All-Rookie Second Team (1992). After a six-year NBA career that saw stops with the Denver Nuggets and Detroit Pistons, Macon took assistant coaching jobs at Temple and Georgia State before landing a head coaching gig at Binghamton College in New York. (Courtesy of the Temple Athletic Department.)

Mike Vreeswyk was named first-team All–Atlantic 10 for 1989, as well as first-team All–Big 5, which went along with his second-team selection the year prior. Vreeswyk is a member of the Big 5 Hall of Fame.

Former Atlantic 10 Player of the Year Eddie Jones is pictured during one of his two stints with the Miami Heat. This autographed photograph shows the former Temple star during his NBA heyday, in a career that saw him play for five teams in 14 years. Jones appeared in three all-star games after being drafted 10th overall by the Los Angeles Lakers in the 1994 NBA draft. While at Temple, Jones won the Robert V. Geasey Trophy in 1994. Temple won the Big 5 title in each of his three seasons.

This schedule features the entire roster of the 1992–1993 Temple women's basketball team. This was a down year for the Owls, as the team finished a disappointing 8-19, including 3-11 in conference play and 2-2 in the Big 5. Featured on this schedule are, from left to right (first row) Maragrite Rougier, Jennifer Linthicum, Chantel Adkins, Sonya Perry, and Rochelle Weaver; (second row) Nikki Inzano, Amy Dittenber, Jennifer Oxley, Kendra Westmoreland, Renee Jones, Mickey Wetzel, and Tamara Davis.

Although he spent his playing career at Penn (winning a Big 5 title in the 1993–1994 season), Dan Leibovitz made most of his Big 5 legacy at Temple, where, as an assistant to John Chaney, he helped coach the Owls to five Big 5 titles. After a two-year stint at Penn, this time as a coach, Leibovitz coached at the professional level for a year before being named the associate commissioner for basketball for the Southeastern Conference.

Lynn Greer stands today as one of the more prolific scorers in both Temple and the Big 5's history. A recipient of the Robert V. Geasey Trophy in 2002, Greer was a two-time All–Atlantic 10 selection and a member of two Big 5 championship squads. After a short stint with the Milwaukee Bucks, Greer found his skills were better suited for the European leagues, where he won championships in Poland, Italy, and Turkey; he also played in Greece, Ukraine, and Russia. His father was drafted by the Phoenix Suns in 1973. (Courtesy of the Temple Athletic Department.)

Embracing his son Jalen (who would go on to a stellar career of his own at Villanova) is Temple legend Rick Brunson. Brunson was a four-year starter for the Owls, who managed to win a Big 5 title (although unofficial) in each of his four seasons. A McDonald's High School All-American, Brunson averaged four points per game in nine NBA seasons. His wife, Sandra, also pictured, was a four-year letter winner for the Temple volleyball team.

Temple's Pepe Sanchez was one of the more unique and successful players in the history of the Big 5. Sanchez never averaged more than six points a game in his time at Temple, yet he managed to claim two Robert V. Geasey Trophies (1999–2000), along with Atlantic 10 Player of the Year honors and a third-team All-American nod. After his Temple days, Sanchez played in the NBA for the 76ers, Hawks, and Pistons. His greatest success, however, was in international competition, where he was a member of the 2004 Argentine squad that won Olympic gold. (Courtesy of the Temple Athletic Department.)

While not all players are destined to make it to the NBA, or even to start, many are fondly remembered for their contributions to their school. This is personified in scrappy Temple guard T.J. DiLeo. Although he only averaged 15 minutes, 2.3 points, and 1 steal per game in his time with the Owls, he always managed to delight the Temple faithful with his hard-nosed and relentless play. A member of three of Temple's record 27 Big 5 championship teams, DiLeo now plays professionally in Germany, where he averages a respectable 10 points, 4 rebounds, and 4 assists a game.

From 2002 to 2006, Temple Owl star Antywane Robinson averaged 12.7 points and 5 rebounds a game, earning second-team All–Atlantic 10 honors as a senior. After going undrafted in 2006, Robinson took his skills to the NBA G League, playing for Sioux Falls. He followed that up by playing in France, Turkey, Italy, Latvia, and Portugal, where he plays today.

Mardy Collins has led a journeyman career since his time at Temple. After winning a Big 5 title in his four seasons as an Owl, he was drafted in the first round by the New York Knicks in the 2006 NBA draft. After stints with the Knicks and Clippers, Collins played professionally in Turkey, China, Israel, Venezuela, Italy, Greece, Poland, France, and Russia.

The co-winner of the 2008 Robert V. Geasey Trophy was Temple's Mark Tyndale. Tyndale played for the Owls from 2004 to 2008, during which time the Owls won two Big 5 titles, both shared with Villanova. A shooting guard, Tyndale averaged over 15 points a game his last two seasons with the Owls, both of which resulted in All–Big 5 selections. A journeyman professional, Tyndale has played for stateside developmental teams in Maine, South Dakota, Iowa, Nevada, and Tennessee, and internationally for clubs in Australia, Germany, Ukraine, Sweden, and Israel. (Courtesy of the Temple Athletic Department.)

Shown here with the Phoenix Suns, Dionte Christmas had a remarkable four-year career as a Temple Owl. A member of one Big 5 championship team, Christmas went undrafted in the 2009 NBA draft. After professional stints in Israel, Turkey, the Czech Republic, Greece, Russia, and Italy, Christmas made his way back to the NBA with the Suns before playing in France, Israel, Greece, and Turkey. He finished his career in the NBA D-League, playing for the Delaware 87ers.

Pictured here in a game against Ohio University is former Temple Owl Muhammad Wilkerson (No. 9). Wilkerson played on two teams that went up against a Big 5 opponent, losing in 2009 to Villanova in double overtime in the Mayor's Cup and leading the Owls to a 31-24 win over the Wildcats in the 2010 Mayor's Cup. Wilkerson left Temple after his junior year, declaring for the NFL draft, where he was a first-round selection (30th overall) by the New York Jets. He has twice been named an NFL All-Pro, following the 2013 and 2015 seasons.

Former Temple Owl Ryan Brooks spent four years on the Temple squad, averaging 14.3 points a game as a senior. He was a member of two Big 5 championship teams before going undrafted in the 2010 NBA draft. Brooks went on to play professionally in Germany, Finland, and France.

One of Temple's 28 Big 5 championships came in the 2011–2012 season, when the Owls stormed to a 24-8 record, a regular-season Atlantic 10 championship, and a 4-1 record in the Big 5 (of note is that Temple split a season series with Saint Joseph's 1-1, as well as the Big 5 title). The women's team finished the season 23-10, with a WNIT berth and a trip to the semifinals. The Owls finished 3-1 in Big 5 play, with wins over Penn, La Salle, and Saint Joseph's, and a loss to Villanova.

This autographed photograph shows the 2011 winner of the Robert V. Geasey Trophy, Lavoy Allen of the Temple Owls. Allen was a four-year starter for the Owls before being selected in the second round (50th overall) by his hometown Philadelphia 76ers. After three years in Philadelphia, Allen was traded to the Indiana Pacers, where he would play until 2017. He remains the all-time leader in rebounds in Temple history. The Owls won two Big 5 titles during his tenure.

The 2013 Robert V. Geasey Trophy winner, Khalif Wyatt, played for four years at Temple, and while his relationship with coach Fran Dunphy was rather contentious at first, the pair blossomed into a touching dynamic that helped Wyatt grow as a player and as a person. Wyatt won three Big 5 titles in his time at Temple as well as an Atlantic 10 Sixth Man of the Year award and an Atlantic 10 Player of the Year honor. Undrafted in the NBA draft, Wyatt played in the summer league for the Philadelphia 76ers before playing in China and Israel, where he still plays today. (Courtesy of the Temple Athletic Department.)

Liacouras Arena is home to the Temple Owls. Constructed around the same time as La Salle's Tom Gola Arena, this arena is named after former Temple president Peter J. Liacouras, who was responsible for securing the funds needed to construct it, albeit at the urging of legendary coach John Chaney. The venue seats 10,200 fans and is one of the tougher road games for Temple opponents. Built at a cost of $73 million, the arena also plays host to concerts, performances, roller derby, and graduation ceremonies.

Five

THE VILLANOVA UNIVERSITY WILDCATS

I grew up a Philadelphia Big 5 fan. I rooted for all the teams in the Big 5 and loved to attend doubleheaders at this wondrous place called the Palestra. The Big 5 teams were each ranked in the top five in the country during a span of 30 years (1955–1985). When my high school team finally made it to the Catholic League playoffs, which were played in the Palestra, I was hooked on going to a Big 5 school. I chose to attend Villanova after much discussion.

My memories of playing in the Big 5 are many, but I will narrow them down to two. The first is a game against our huge rival, Saint Joseph's, my senior year at Villanova. Saint Joseph's was the heavy favorite, ranked in the top 20 in the country. Traditionally, for both schools, this contest was a big game. Frequently, the team that was supposed to win ended up losing. This game remained true to form: We beat Saint Joseph's in overtime for a huge win.

The second memory was against Penn, but it was not at the Palestra and it was not considered an official Big 5 game. It was played in the Eastern Regional final in Raleigh, North Carolina. Penn was undefeated, second in the country and a heavy favorite; we were playing well but not ranked very highly. We played out of our minds and beat Penn 90-47 to go to the Final Four.

—Dr. Edward Hastings
Former player, Villanova (BA, Villanova, 1973)

(Author's Note: Dr. Edward "Ed" Hastings played for Villanova from 1970 to 1973. After averaging 11 points in his senior season, Hastings went on to receive a doctorate in spirituality. Today, he is a professor in the graduate theology program at Villanova.)

Perhaps no player stands out more in the history of Villanova basketball than Paul Arizin. Although his career was before the Big 5, his play made Villanova a serious threat in Philadelphia and helped spark rivalries with other area schools. After an All-American career as a Wildcat, Arizin was the No. 1 pick in the NBA draft by his hometown Warriors. He was named Rookie of the Year, made 10 all-star teams, won an NBA championship, and was inducted into both the professional and college basketball halls of fame. Arizin was a member of the NBA 50th Anniversary team.

Big 5 and Villanova Hall of Famer Wali Jones is pictured during his time with his hometown Philadelphia 76ers. Jones was a dominant force in Big 5 play, twice winning the Robert V. Geasey Trophy in his time with the Wildcats. Villanova won two Big 5 titles during his time, and he was drafted by the Detroit Pistons in 1964. He played for the Bullets, 76ers, Bucks, and Pistons in his NBA career, winning an NBA title in 1967.

Shown here playing for the ABA's New Jersey Nets is Villanova Hall of Famer Bill Melchionni. Although the Wildcats were unable to win a Big 5 title during his tenure, Melchionni did win the Robert V. Geasey Trophy in 1966, his senior season. His career in the NBA started with his hometown Philadelphia 76ers before he jumped to the New Jersey Nets of the upstart ABA. He won one NBA and two ABA championships before retiring, and his number, 25, is retired by the Nets.

Villanova Hall of Famer Keith Herron's four-year career (1974–1978) saw the Wildcats take home two Big 5 titles, in his sophomore and senior seasons. After leaving Villanova as its all-time scorer (a record that would stand for 19 years), Herron played for the Hawks, Pistons, and Cavaliers after being drafted by Portland. He was an All-American, All-NIT, and all Big 5 selection and is in the Big 5 Hall of Fame.

On October 12, 1979, Chris Ford made the first three-point shot in the history of the NBA, for the Boston Celtics. Before that, he was a four-year starter for the Villanova Wildcats from 1969 to 1972. He won the Robert V. Geasey Trophy in 1972, although the Wildcats never won any Big 5 titles in his career. Ford played for Detroit and Boston in the NBA, winning a title with the Celtics in 1981 before embarking on an 18-year coaching career that netted him two more titles.

Shown here with the Chicago Bulls, Rory Sparrow was a pivotal four-year letter winner for the Villanova Wildcats. He was one of the most clutch players in Wildcat history, making game-winning shots on at least 10 occasions in his four-year career. After leading the Wildcats to one Big 5 title, Sparrow played for New Jersey, Atlanta, New York, Chicago, Miami, Sacramento, and Los Angeles in the NBA. He is still known today for his philanthropic efforts.

Until the 1984–1985 season, the 1970–1971 Villanova Wildcats represented the peak of accomplishment for the team in national play. A top-20 squad for much of the season, the Wildcats made an improbable run in the NCAA tournament, which included a 90-47 upset over previously undefeated (and Big 5 rival) Penn. The Wildcats made it all the way to the NCAA championship game, losing to the John Wooden–led UCLA Bruins. This runner-up finish was vacated by the Wildcats after it was discovered that the tournament's Most Outstanding Player, Howard Porter (pictured), had signed with an agent before the tournament. The forfeit left Penn as one of the few undefeated teams in history not to be named NCAA champions. (Courtesy of Villanova Athletics.)

Under the leadership of coach Rollie Massimino, the 1981–1982 Villanova squad stormed to a 24-8 record, including an 11-3 record in Big East play and the Big East title. Although the season did not include a Big 5 title, as the team stumbled to a 2-2 record in Big 5 play, with wins over Penn and La Salle and losses to Temple and Saint Joseph's, the team advanced to the Elite Eight. Pictured here is senior forward Aaron Howard, who averaged 7.9 points for the Wildcats.

John Pinone's number, 45, was retired by Villanova in 1995. A Wildcat from 1979 to 1983, Pinone helped lay the foundation for the Wildcats' success in the 1980s. He won three straight Robert V. Geasey Trophies from 1981 to 1983, and led the Wildcats to two Big 5 titles. He was drafted by the Atlanta Hawks in the 1983 draft and spent a season playing for them before carving out an incredible 10-year career in Spain.

By Villanova's lofty standards, the 1983–1984 season was mediocre at best. The Wildcats made their way to a rather lackluster 19-12 record, although their 12-4 conference record was good enough for third place in the Big East. Their record was 2-2 in the Big 5, with wins over Penn and Saint Joseph's and losses to La Salle and Temple. The Big 5 title was shared that season between those two teams, who both finished 3-1 in Big 5 play. Featured on this card is senior guard Frank "Happy" Dobbs, who averaged 10.3 points per game.

Shown here with Pres. Ronald Reagan at the White House, the 1984–1985 Villanova Wildcats were one of the greatest Cinderella stories in the history of college basketball. Although the team sported a 25-10 record (including 9-7 in Big East play, which was only good enough for fourth place), the team, led by legendary coach Rollie Massimino and the likes of Ed Pinckney, Dwayne McClain, and Howard Pressley, made an improbable run to the national championship game, where, in a match dubbed "The Perfect Game," they managed to shock top-ranked Georgetown (who finished with a 35-3 record) by a final tally of 66-64. The Wildcats remain the lowest seed to win the NCAA tournament. They won the Big 5 that year as well, finishing 4-0. (Courtesy of Villanova Athletics.)

Many members of the 1984–1985 national champion Villanova Wildcats have moved on to greater success. Ed Pickney is now an assistant coach with the Denver Nuggets. Dwayne McClain worked in the financial services industry after a professional career that spanned 12 seasons. Gary McLain is a motivational speaker for TeamRoc Sports. Other members have moved on to television, radio, coaching, construction, petroleum, and the FBI. The success of this team, it seems, translated well off the court.

VILLANOVA 1985-86

1985 NCAA NATIONAL CHAMPIONS

A year after their miraculous run to the NCAA championship, the 1985–1986 Villanova Wildcats found themselves having another strong, if uneven, season. The Wildcats finished 23-14, including a 10-6 record in the Big East, for a fourth-place regular season finish. They also advanced to both the second round of the Big East and the NCAA tournament. In Big 5 play, the Wildcats finished 2-2, with wins over Penn and La Salle and losses to co-champions Temple and Saint Joseph's.

This autographed photograph shows Harold Jensen, who spent four seasons with the Villanova Wildcats, leading them to a national title and a Big 5 championship. Although drafted by the Cleveland Cavaliers, Jensen never played in the NBA. He was, however, a two-time Academic All-American. He was voted into the Big 5 Hall of Fame in 1995.

The Big 5 is not the only inter-conference that Villanova has participated in. Aside from the City 6, which includes Drexel, Villanova participated in three ACC–Big East challenges from 1989 to 1991. This postcard from the 1989 Challenge, which simulates the program, shows a faux ticket stub from Villanova's December 7 tilt against Virginia, a game they lost 73-65. The Wildcats stumbled to an 18-15 record that season, although they were runners-up in the Big 5, with their only loss coming to La Salle.

Although the full Big 5 went on hiatus from 1991 to 1999, the Philadelphia teams still scheduled occasional games against one another, with the team that had the best record still being awarded the unofficial title of Big 5 champion. While Villanova powered its way to a 20-12 record in the 1993–1994 season, they finished 1-1 in Big 5 play, losing to Temple (co-champions along with Penn) and beating La Salle. Pictured here is sophomore guard Kerry Kittles, who averaged nearly 20 points per game that season. Kittles played nine years in the NBA for the New Jersey Nets and Los Angeles Clippers before taking an assistant coaching job at Princeton.

Shown here signing an autograph for a fan is Villanova legend and current Boston Celtics assistant coach Alvin Williams. Although the Wildcats only managed one Big 5 title during Williams's tenure (1996–1997), he was still a great success, earning first-team All–Big East honors in 1997. The Portland Trail Blazers took Williams in the second round (47th overall) of the 1997 NBA draft. Williams went on to a successful 10-year NBA career with the Trail Blazers, Raptors, and Clippers before joining the coaching ranks.

Although Tim Thomas only spent one year with the Wildcats, it was an impactful one. The Wildcats won the 1996–1997 Big 5 title, and Thomas went on to be drafted seventh overall by the New Jersey Nets, who immediately traded him to the Philadelphia 76ers. Thomas spent 13 years in the NBA, playing for Philadelphia, New York, Milwaukee, Chicago, Phoenix, Los Angeles, and Dallas.

Villanova alum and current Pistons assistant coach Malik Allen is one of the few players in history who can claim four Big 5 titles. Allen nonetheless went undrafted in the 2000 NBA draft. However, he earned his way into the league as a reliable hand, spending time with Miami, Charlotte, Chicago, New Jersey, Dallas, Milwaukee, Denver, and Orlando before retiring in 2014.

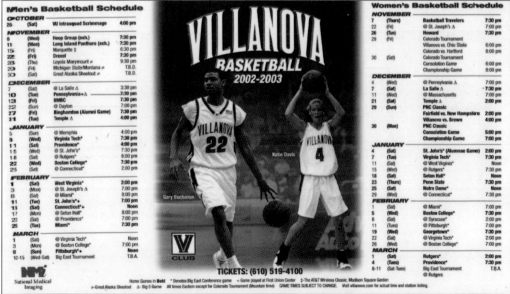

The 2002–2003 schedule for both men's and women's basketball at Villanova features Gary Buchanan, who was twice Big 5 Player of the Week and currently plays professional basketball in Ukraine, and Katie Davis, a four-year letterwoman for the Wildcats, who led her team to a second-round NCAA appearance in her senior season.

Three-time NBA All-Star and former Villanova Wildcat Kyle Lowry is pictured playing for the Toronto Raptors. In his short stint with the Wildcats, Lowry was named once to both the All–Big East and All–Big 5 teams. He was drafted in the first round (24th overall) by the Memphis Grizzlies and has played for the Grizzlies, Rockets, and Raptors during his career. He also earned a gold medal at the 2016 Olympics as a member of Team USA.

Randy Foye's college career was riddled with accolades: he was a consensus first-team All-American in 2006 as well as the Big East Player of the Year and winner of the Robert V. Geasey Trophy. He was drafted seventh overall by the Boston Celtics, although draft night trades sent him first to Portland and then to Minnesota.

Former Villanova star Allan Ray led the Wildcats to the Elite Eight in his senior season (2005–2006), earning second-team All-American honors as the Wildcats finished with a 28-5 record. The Wildcats won two Big 5 titles during his tenure (2004–2005, 2005–2006) before he graduated and headed to the NBA as an undrafted signee of the Boston Celtics. Ray played one NBA season before embarking on a professional career that has led him to Italy, Slovenia, France, Germany, Croatia, and Turkey.

Dante Cunningham was a four-year starter for the Wildcats. In 2005–2006, he was named the Big 5 Rookie of the Year. That season, he set a career high in blocks (four) against La Salle. After leading the Wildcats to the 2008–2009 Final Four, he took home Villanova's Most Outstanding Player award as well as Most Improved Player in the Big East. He was a second-round draft pick for the Portland Trail Blazers and currently plays for the New Orleans Pelicans.

The 2008–2009 season was a great success for the women's squad by historical standards. The Wildcats finished with a 19-14 record, earning an eight seed in the NCAA tournament, where they fell to Utah by a score of 60-30. Senior forward Laura Kurz (pictured) earned Big 5 Player of the Year honors.

From 2009 to 2012, Maalik Wayns manned the point for the Villanova Wildcats. He earned Big East All-Freshman team honors in 2010 and second-team All–Big East honors in 2012 before jumping to the NBA. After stints in Philadelphia and Los Angeles, Wayns played for professional teams in Puerto Rico, Italy, Russia, Israel, and Spain.

Although Darrun Hillard came up one season short of winning a national championship at Villanova, his four-year legacy cannot be questioned. He led the Wildcats to two Big 5 titles in his career and earned all–Big East and All-American honors. After being drafted by the Detroit Pistons in the 2015 NBA draft, he spent two years in the Motor City before being traded to Houston, then the Clippers, in a matter of two days. A day later he was released, only to sign with San Antonio, his current team.

The Villanova Wildcats won their second NCAA championship after the 2015–2016 season, once again in thrilling fashion. Under the leadership of coach Jay Wright, the Wildcats finished the season 33-5, which included winning the Big East regular season championship game. Earning a two seed, the Wildcats beat North Carolina in the national championship game 77-74 on a last-second three-pointer by Kris Jenkins. The Wildcats also finished the season 4-0 in Big 5 play, earning their third consecutive Big 5 title. (Courtesy of Villanova Athletics.)

Villanova center Daniel Ochefu came to the Wildcats by way of Baltimore, Maryland, and was the starting center on the 2015–2016 Villanova national championship team. Of more importance are the three Big 5 championships the Wildcats won during his last three seasons on the team, sweeping the rest of the field each season. An honorable mention All–Big East player in 2016, Ochefu went undrafted in the NBA, choosing to sign a free agent contract with the Washington Wizards. His contributions off the bench helped Washington make the playoffs in 2017.

Villanova swingman Ryan Arcidiacono was named Most Outstanding Player in the NCAA championship game in 2016. The game, won on a last-second buzzer beater (one that Arcidiacono assisted on), gave the Wildcats their second national championship. Arcidiacono won three Big 5 titles in his time at Villanova and finished with a 14-2 overall record in Big 5 play. Undrafted in the 2016 NBA draft, he signed a developmental deal with the San Antonio Spurs, currently playing for its developmental league team, the Austin Spurs.

Villanova forward Kris Jenkins came to Villanova by way of Gonzaga College High School in Washington, DC. He will be most remembered by Wildcat fans for sinking the game-winning three-pointer against North Carolina in the national championship game on April 4, 2016. Villanova entered the tournament as a two seed and was ranked seventh overall before the tournament. Jenkins finished his Villanova career 16-0 against Big 5 opponents, as Villanova won four straight league titles under his watch. Undrafted in the 2017 draft, Jenkins signed a free agent deal with the Washington Wizards.

This photograph shows two members of the 2016–2017 Big 5 champion Wildcats, Dylan Painter and Josh Hart. Painter is a sophomore who played in 23 games for the Wildcats as a freshman, averaging a point and 1.35 rebounds on a deep Villanova bench. Hart, a four-year player for the Wildcats, was one of the anchors on the 2015–2016 national championship squad. He averaged 18.9 points and 6.4 rebounds as a senior, earning first-team All-American and Big East Player of the Year honors before being drafted in the first round (30th overall) by the Utah Jazz, who promptly traded him to the Los Angeles Lakers.

DISCOVER THOUSANDS OF LOCAL HISTORY BOOKS FEATURING MILLIONS OF VINTAGE IMAGES

Arcadia Publishing, the leading local history publisher in the United States, is committed to making history accessible and meaningful through publishing books that celebrate and preserve the heritage of America's people and places.

Find more books like this at
www.arcadiapublishing.com

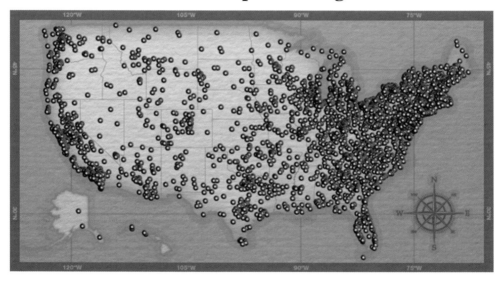

Search for your hometown history, your old stomping grounds, and even your favorite sports team.

MADE IN THE USA